1

A Pet's Life

Hamsters

Anita Ganeri

Heinemann
LIBRARY

www.heinemannlibrary.co.uk
Visit our website to find out more information about Heinemann Library books.

To order:
☎ Phone +44 (0) 1865 888066
🖷 Fax +44 (0) 1865 314091
🖳 Visit www.heinemannlibrary.co.uk

Heinemann Library is an imprint of Capstone Global Library Limited, a company incorporated in England and Wales having its registered office at 7 Pilgrim Street, London, EC4V 6LB – Registered company number: 6695582

"Heinemann" is a registered trademark of Pearson Education Limited, under licence to Capstone Global Library Limited.

Text © Capstone Global Library Limited
Second edition first published in hardback and paperback in 2009
The moral rights of the proprietor have been asserted.

Edited by Charlotte Guillain and Harriet Milles
Designed by Joanna Hinton-Malivoire
Picture research by Elizabeth Alexander and Rebecca Sodergren
Production by Victoria Fitzgerald
Originated by Chroma Graphics (Overseas) Pte. Ltd
Printed and bound in China by South China Printing Company Ltd.

ISBN 978 04311 7791 5 (hardback)
13 12 11 10 09
10 9 8 7 6 5 4 3 2 1

ISBN 978 0 4311 7798 4 (paperback)
13 12 11 10 09
10 9 8 7 6 5 4 3 2 1

British Library Cataloguing in Publication Data
Ganeri, Anita, 1961-
  Hamsters. - 2nd ed. - (A pet's life) (Heinemann first library)
  1. Hamsters as pets - Juvenile literature
  I. Title
  636.9'356
A full catalogue record for this book is available from the British Library.

Acknowledgements
We would like to thank the following for permission to reproduce photographs:
Alamy p. 7 (© Maximilian Weinzierl); Ardea p. 6 (I R Beames); Armitage Pet Care p. 10; © Capstone Global Library Ltd. pp. 11, 12, 15, 16, 17, 18, 19, 21, 22, 23, 25, 26, 27 (Haddon Davies), 20 (Trevor Clifford), 8, 9, 13, 14 (Tudor Photography); Dorling Kindersley p. 4; NaturePl.com p. 5 (Barry Bland); Photolibrary/OSF p. 24 (Renee Stockdale-AA).

Cover photograph of a golden hamster reproduced with permission of FLPA (Michael Krabs/Imagebroker).

The publishers would like to thank Rob Lee for his assistance in the preparation of this book.

Every effort has been made to contact copyright holders of material reproduced in this book. Any omissions will be rectified in subsequent printings if notice is given to the publishers.

Disclaimer

Contents

Any words appearing in the text in bold, **like this**, are explained in the Glossary.

What do hamsters look like?

Hamsters are small and furry. They look a lot like large mice. The most popular type is the golden hamster. It gets its name from the colour of its fur.

Most golden hamsters have short, silky fur.

This picture shows the different parts of a hamster's body. You can see what each part is used for.

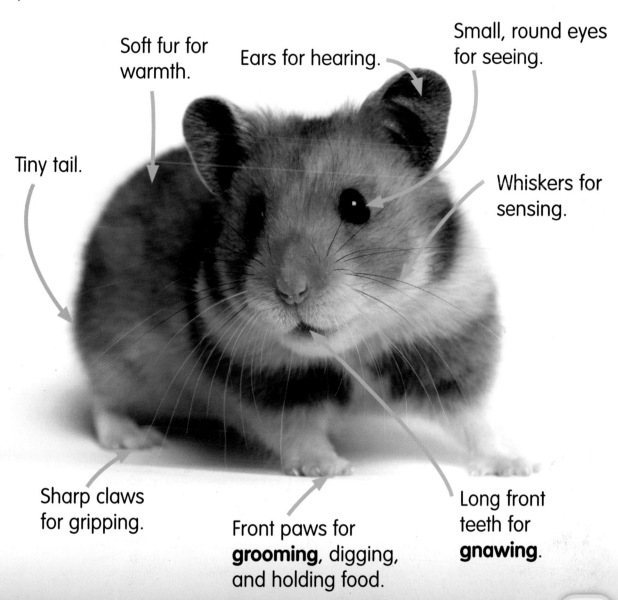

Soft fur for warmth.

Ears for hearing.

Small, round eyes for seeing.

Tiny tail.

Whiskers for sensing.

Sharp claws for gripping.

Front paws for **grooming**, digging, and holding food.

Long front teeth for **gnawing**.

Hamster babies

Baby hamsters are called **cubs**. A mother hamster has about five to seven cubs in a **litter**. The mother hamster feeds her cubs on milk.

Cubs are born with no fur and with their eyes closed.

At six weeks old, the cubs start to play and fight.

The cubs are old enough to leave their mother when they are about six weeks old. Then they are ready to become pets.

Choosing your hamster

You can buy a hamster from a good pet shop or from a hamster breeder. **Animal shelters** often have hamsters that need good homes.

Pick a lively hamster. A shy or nervous-looking hamster may not be very well.

Choose a plump hamster with soft, shiny fur. See that its skin is free from sores or bald patches. Check that its bottom is dry and clean.

A healthy hamster's eyes, ears, teeth, mouth, and nose should be clean.

Fitting out your cage

Hamsters are very lively. They like to run and climb. Your hamster needs a large cage to live in, with a snug **nest box** inside to sleep in.

Stacking cages have several floors to explore.

Your hamster's nest box should be filled with shredded tissue paper for bedding. Put the cage in a warm place, out of bright sunlight and away from draughts.

Put a layer of wood shavings on the floor of the cage.

Welcome home

You can bring your hamster home in a small cardboard box. At home, put your hamster in its cage. Leave it alone for a few hours to settle in.

Make sure the box has holes in it so that your hamster has air to breathe.

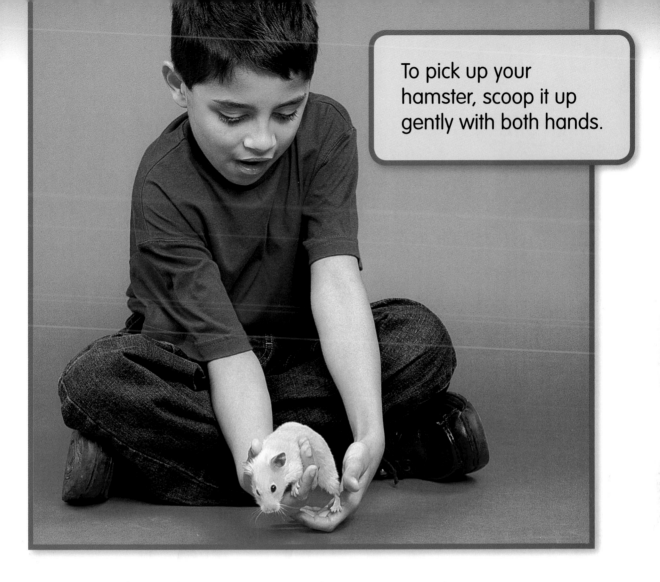

To pick up your hamster, scoop it up gently with both hands.

Be gentle when you pick up your hamster. Move slowly and quietly. Otherwise your hamster may get frightened and try to bite you.

Play time

Hamsters need lots of exercise. Put an exercise wheel in the cage. Jam jars, cardboard tubes and climbing frames also make good toys.

The exercise wheel must be solid so that your hamster does not trap its feet.

If you let your pet out of its cage, shut all the doors and windows. Hamsters can run very fast and are small and tricky to find.

Let your hamster climb from one of your hands to the other.

Feeding time

Hamsters like to eat seeds, nuts, and grains. You can buy a mixture from a pet shop. Hamsters like to store food in **pouches** in their cheeks. They eat it later.

You can also feed your hamster some fresh fruit and vegetables.

You should feed your hamster once a day in the evening. Put the food in a heavy dish so that it does not tip over.

Make sure that your pet always has fresh water to drink. Buy your hamster a **drip feed** water bottle.

Cleaning the cage

You can help your hamster to stay healthy by keeping its cage clean. Every day, take away any **droppings** and bits of old food.

Wash out the food bowl and water bottle every day.

Put some fresh bedding in the **nest box**.

Every week, give the whole cage a thorough clean. Change the layer of wood shavings on the floor. Don't forget to wash your hands after cleaning your hamster's cage.

Growing up

Hamsters grow up very quickly. When a golden hamster is fully grown, it will measure about 10 cm long and weigh about 100 g.

A hamster can easily fit in your hands.

Golden hamsters like to live on their own.

If you put two golden hamsters in the same cage, they may fight each other. Never keep a hamster in a cage with other animals.

A healthy hamster

Your hamster will stay healthy if you care for it properly. But hamsters can catch colds and flu from people. If you think your hamster looks unwell, take it to a vet.

A wet tail can be a sign that your hamster is ill.

A hamster's front teeth grow all the time. If your hamster's teeth grow too long, it may not be able to eat properly.

Give your hamster a wooden **gnawing** block to wear its teeth down.

Your pet hamster

Hamsters are fun to keep as pets and are quite easy to look after. But you must be a good pet owner and care for your hamster properly.

You need time to feed your hamster, play with it, and keep it clean.

If you go on holiday, make sure that someone looks after your hamster. It is best to take your hamster to a friend's house. Or ask someone to call in every day.

Your hamster must always have food, fresh water, and clean bedding.

Old age

If you look after your hamster, it may live for about two to three years. As it gets older, it might lose some fur and put on weight.

An old hamster might need special care.

It can be very upsetting when your pet dies. Try not to be too sad. Just remember the happy times you shared together.

Caring for your hamster will help you learn how to treat animals properly.

Useful tips

- Hamsters wake up at night. So put the cage in a place where it will not disturb you.

- Don't wake your hamster up in the day to play. It might bite you.

- Keep the cage out of reach of cats and other pets.

- Hamsters clean their fur with their front paws. But you need to brush long-haired hamsters gently every day with a soft toothbrush.

- Don't line the cage with newspaper. The printed ink is **poisonous** to your hamster.

- Let your hamster sniff your fingers. It will get to know you by how you smell.

- If the room you keep your hamster in gets colder than 10 degrees, it may fall asleep.

Fact file

- Wild hamsters live in the desert.

- Wild hamsters spend the day sleeping in **burrows** under the ground. This keeps them cool.

- All pet golden hamsters come from one hamster family. They were found in the desert in Syria in 1930.

- The name "hamster" comes from a German word which means "hoarder". This is because hamsters **hoard** food in their cheeks.

- An adult hamster needs about 10 g of food a day. That's about a teaspoonful.

- Hamsters are short-sighted. They cannot see very well.

Glossary

animal shelter place where lost or unwanted animals are looked after

burrow hole in the ground

cub baby hamster

drip feeder bottle that lets water slowly drip out. It is fixed to the hamster's cage.

droppings hamsters' poo

gnaw chew and bite

groom gently brush and clean your hamster's fur. Hamsters also groom themselves.

hoard store or keep for later

litter group of hamster babies

nest box box for your hamster to sleep in

poisonous something that can cause illness or death

pouches spaces inside a hamster's cheeks where it stores food

More information

Books to read

Read and Learn: Hamsters, Jennifer Blizin Gillis (Heinemann Library, 2004)

My Pet: Hamsters and Gerbils, Honor Head (Belitha Press, 2000)

RSPCA Pet Guide: Care for your Hamster (Collins, 2004)

Websites

www.rspca.org.uk
The website of The Royal Society for the Prevention of Cruelty to Animals in Britain.

www.pethealthcare.co.uk
Information about caring for first pets.

www.petlink.com.au
Information about being a good pet owner.

Index